The Lines

Also by Eli Wilde

Cruel
Four Days (with 'Anna DeVine)

Writing as Frank Lambert

Napoloeon Xylophone
Xyz

The Lines

Eli Wilde

Matador
9 Priory Business Park,
Wistow Road, Kibworth Beauchamp,
Leicestershire. LE8 0RX
Tel: (+44) 116 279 2299
Fax: (+44) 116 279 2277
Email: books@troubador.co.uk
Web: www.troubador.co.uk/matador

ISBN 978 1784620 226

British Library Cataloguing in Publication Data.
A catalogue record for this book is available from the British Library.

Typeset in Minion Pro by Troubador Publishing Ltd, Leicester, UK
Printed and bound in the UK by TJ International, Padstow, Cornwall

Matador is an imprint of Troubador Publishing Ltd

Until you speak

Wild Flower

In the open field,
past the broken rickshaw,

I saw you lying on your back
staring at the sky.

Clouds move so fast,
you said, as I approached.

Laying down beside you
I tried to see what you meant,

but taking in the scent of wild peony,
when your hair blew on the breeze,

clouds held no meaning
as I closed my eyes to the sky

and listened to the breeze
racing through the long grass.

Morning Fog

I wanted to lick your shoulder
along its length, until I reached your neck,

and your fingers,
I wanted them inside my mouth,

with you staring at me,
giving me that look.

I thought I understood then,
the meaning in your eyes,

until you left and I realised
I no longer knew you at all.

Allure Velvet

Your hair tied back, strands
hang loose around your neck.

I look up, staring at your naked breasts
in the mirror

as you paint your lips
deep red, glossy Chanel.

Bending into your neck
I take in your scent

without touching,
move across to the tip

of your shoulder
where I gently kiss.

You close your eyes
and continue to colour your lips

until they are smudged,
until you begin to weep.

Disturbing Beauty

In a way it's a matter of existence,
you and me naked, sitting on the bed

holding hands, facing each other,
I wonder what you see in my eyes.

You lean into me
bite my lip, and lean back.

Your scent fills my space
and I squeeze your hands

seeing something no longer real,
now that I no longer exist for you.

Until You Speak

Listening carefully to your silence,
its beauty,

I know it doesn't happen by chance,
always, it is carefully thought out.

It serves a purpose,
perhaps one you don't intend.

I am on your mind
even if only to ignore,

and that means more to me
than anything else I feel.

You see, nothing is ever real for me
until I share it with you,

and all we share these days
is your muted breath.

Mistake

We turn to black, weeping tears forsaken,
never asking why.

I don't think I was ever meant to be,
and I'm sorry, for breezing into your life.

If I could erase the time I spent with you
from your memory, I would

and I'm sorry about your brother
I never meant for him to lose his mind.

Never meant for him
to come between you and me.

Mixed Blood

You never answer my messages,
why would you?

I think I am dying
an unhurried, burning death.

I tell myself each day
to stop thinking of you,

every minute of every day
how foolish I am.

Waning here alone
like a castaway, forsaken

with only scraps to feed upon,
memories of you

vivid and resolute
like echoes of psychosis.

Emotion is Illusion

I need to get away from the light,
the dark.

Feelings aren't real
they only exist in the past,

like these memories
I fake each day with you

they fail to comprehend truth.
Only when you say my name,

when you whisper my name
against my skin

only moments like these are real
and now that you are gone

everything is illusion
everything is nothing.

Unintentional

We never spoke
just listened to music

drinking Pinot,
darkly contemplating.

Breathing in your scent
as we made the sound of love.

I wanted to tell you,
but you came and the moment went.

So I remained silent
as sleep overtook us

and the next morning we parted
just like you said we always would.

Circles

Leaving regret behind in Paris,
the deserted road west was painfully lonely.

Night-time driving isolated me further
and thoughts quickly sank into circles.

Slipping a disc into the player, lyrical wit
began to take my mind off the city,

but not you, whose sweet scent lingered
as if you were still by my side.

When the edge of a cloud came into view,
I was suddenly caught in the beauty of the moment,

and feeling; for the first time in a long time,
I switched off the main beam.

A few thousand revolutions up the road
it finally happened.

The full moon emerged from behind the cloud
and I fell into sublime reflection

as the luminous road edified
and led me to a new beginning.

Guess Who Died

It lulls me
the way a train moves

and when I listen to music
with my bloodstream full of alcohol

it pulls me into the zone
where I remember

all those things I forgot
before I ever met you.

Until Morning

The train pulled in slowly,
alongside mine.

I stared across at her
through window and window.

She was biting a pen,
looking at something on the table.

She suddenly turned around,
staring at me.

Her eyes were empty,
and she must have seen the same,

because she continued to stare
deep into mine,

until her train pulled away
taking her nowhere.

While I remained behind
waiting for my train to do the same.

Spidery, Amorphous

You inside my head,
your taste, inside my mouth.

I pour another drink,
listen to another song.

My mind wanders
always back to you.

Paris burning bright,
a room in a hotel.

Music from the bar downstairs;
random blues and jazz.

Images sear
on top of the bed, the floor,

your face in my hands,
your tongue inside my mouth

and your skin scent,
no more than a dream today.

Later, we slept, then breakfast;
silver spoons and white cups,

on top of the bed, unaware,
a kiss is never simply a kiss.

A Sound Like

The sun shines, yet still
it rains, only just.

I can't hear it, but I see speckles
against the carriage window.

Listening to them,
through noise cancelling headphones,

I want to switch them off
to experience something else.

Something melodic and natural
now streaming down the glass.

It makes me feel, feel again you,
afternoon tea in Paris.

Wet and melodic
like a sound beauty would make.

But I keep stalling these days,
as I try to remember how to forget your name.

Cadence

I thought I heard your voice
in the park, this afternoon.

It was overcast, but when the sun broke out
the air burned like Paris in summer.

I left work early,
too distracted to function that way,

and found myself in the park by chance,
only realising I was there, after the sunken garden.

Turning around at the sound
I saw it wasn't you.

She smiled, as if she knew me
and maybe I did the same.

I don't remember how I got back home,
or when I started to write these lines.

And listening to your voice now,
those words you said to me, finally,

I want to turn around again
to change everything left unsaid.

In the Darkness

It is wrong
that we should be together.

Yet here I ache
for your touch, your presence.

Pressing my hand
against the carriage window,

I stare
through splayed fingers

at the darkness
consuming everything outside.

Specks of light glint
before the train speeds them away

and I close my eyes,
yet my reflection stares back,

waiting
for a light that is never set to shine.

For Me, For You

He bites his nails, or maybe
the skin around them,

all the time, this dusty old man
sitting next to me, sometimes reading,

sometimes sipping coffee,
one time eating a bacon roll.

I stare out of the window opposite
listening to Santa Fe,

framing images inside my mind
how the landscape changes day-by-day.

Each reflection a different season
depending upon the time of day light,

the unpredictable weather
or a window neglected and unclean.

And you, so far away
how have you changed since?

No matter the light, the climate,
or whichever window I gaze through

you always look the same to me,
shade inside my dreams.

The Secret Room of Velvet

Like raindrops on the sea
I could not hear your voice,

but I saw your eyes
and knew your words by heart.

Remembering another night
when I wanted to put your fingers

into my mouth
to tell you how you made me feel,

I left without a word,
turning my back on sorrow.

And last night there was rain
against the window,

I heard it in my sleep
like a dream shared with the breeze.

Listen Now

I wish I could delete my past,
all of it forsaken.

Every mocking occurrence,
each and every lie.

And while I'm dreaming myopic,
while I'm psyching out,

maybe just by chance,
my future is finished too.

Your name suddenly comes to mind
and I can't stop saying it over,

over and over again
in the friendly here and now.

Knowing that while I speak,
we were always wrong for each other.

Electronica

Unless we stay young forever,
our dreams will always look back,

and how I tried, how I tried,
until the past took you with gentle hands

to fade away in reminiscence,
in my eyes, my eyes.

Afterwards we remained silent
as I held the future in my palms,

a ghost and a shadow
where all I heard was noise.

Do You Trust?

The scent of your sweat, on the dance floor,
and the music, beat, beat, beat.

I will not falter,
taking in your movements, your look.

And the music, again,
opening doorways inside my mind.

Your arm brushes against mine
and I want to taste your tongue.

Eyes closed, eyes open,
you awaken inside my dream.

Please keep them away,
don't let them touch me.

Details

Tall trees still,
leafless and grey.

And this bottled water,
stale inside my mouth.

I wonder if you would see the same,
taste the same,

if you were beside me now
gazing through the carriage window.

Tall trees naked and compressed
blur side-by-side alone

as they reach skywards
only ever to find each other.

And your taste,
your tongue inside my mouth

not here, not now,
yet always on my mind.

Come Back, Come Back

Music does not sound the same
and this taste inside my mouth

so unfamiliar,
I've never been here before.

The train rolls from side-to-side
and I stare out of the window,

at sunlight burning through mist
as it reveals broken silhouettes,

memories resurfacing,
incomplete and affecting.

Do you see the same things I see?
Do you see stars burning in the night-time sky?

Before You Open Your Eyes

Autumn sun
shining through the grime,

through the carriage window,
onto my face.

A favourite season, once,
somewhere in the past.

Now there is only grime
speckled across a dead face.

The Lines

Too much time to think,
to watch and stare amour.

You in another country,
her across the aisle.

And now I feel drowsy
watching the lines move static,

the stones in-between them blur,
buff and diesel like a stream imagined.

When the sun breaks through,
its glare reflecting from line to eye

I think about you again,
turning my attention to her.

How her eyes look at nothing
as if nothing is all she sees.

What She Did to Me

She sat next to me
on the train,

wanting to talk,
smiling, laughing finer points.

I spoke and smiled back
in a vacant kind of way.

Almost convincing myself,
as her elbow touched mine

– her perfume and voice too,
maybe it was over.

Staring at her painted red nails
I thought about you

scratching along my spine
as you bite into my shoulder.

The Moon on its Way

Listening to the sea
through the open hotel window,

the distant sound of traffic,
a woman moving around next door.

She turns on her music –
'Gold in the Air of Summer'

and I can hardly believe
she would play that song.

Lying on the bed,
staring at the ceiling

I try to visualise her,
not her looks, more how a woman

who listens to the music we shared
would move around in her room.

Then I picture you,
and she fades, her music too,

as I close my eyes and hear nothing
but the crash of waves outside.

Burgess Hill

Sunshine through the trees,
flashing by,

past the grime
of the train window.

Winter countryside vista
black and white, indecipherable.

Grey images remain inside my head
like old, tattered photographs.

Bygone days revisited
of you and I forsaken.

Tortufo Limoncello

Lemon ice cream,
a soft liqueur centre

coated with crushed meringue,
you sitting opposite.

Sipping amaretto
on ice.

Watching me intently,
one spoonful at a time,

refusing me the choice
of drinking cappuccino.

Later, in the chill night-time air,
sitting by the beach,

you kiss me;
almond-coated lips

with a curious tongue
exploring limoncello

while I close my eyes
to everything but your taste.

Reading

Watching you through the gap between seat
and swaying train window,

every now and then your features change
as the words within the book spark response.

Concern upon your face one moment,
empathy sparkling in your eyes the next.

When humour flickers across your mischievous
upturned mouth, I smile and more.

I want to get to know you
once you close the book and I stop reading.

No Big Truth

She pressed her lips gently,
– homesick.

I closed my eyes.
When I opened them,

it had stopped raining
but the trees swayed forlornly

and my eyes
drooped closed, unchallenged,

as green blurred past, wet and unmoving
but for the breeze.

She kissed me again
gently on each eyelid

as I slept, listening to rain
that hadn't yet started to fall.

Reminisce

I stopped caressing you,
just for a moment.

Staring at your ankles,
your calf, the back of your knee.

And leaning into you
I breathed in your skin scent,

from your shoulder,
to your neck, your cheek.

You smiled in your sleep
and I touched your hair,

stroking, until I too fell,
only to be awakened,

later, by the breeze
coming through the carriage window.

Sadness and Beauty

I think it is the sadness of parting,
yes, it must be that.

If I had allowed it to consume me
at the time, maybe.

The train stops abruptly,
as if someone has pulled the cord

and I spill hot coffee over my knees,
it scorches pain beautifully.

The almond croissant
lays half-eaten on the floor.

You in Paris,
me in Brighton,

how your absence
continues to burn inside.

The Morning is Bad

I want to go back,
of course I never do.

Tea each morning without you
hurts like hell.

And I water down gin
telling myself it makes a difference.

I am not in love,
just visiting this solitary place

missing you like hell,
especially in the mornings;

waking up to a new day
that always stays the same.

And at night-time,
at night-time I die.

Still Life

How long is it
since I last heard your voice?

Still, I know you,
how you stand by the window

in the morning
with the sun shining in your hair

as you place the glass
next to your lips,

drinking the water
with your eyes closed.

When you are finished
you open them

and stare at me
even though I am not there.

About the Possibilities

Chill night air
against my skin.

Menthol filter
between my lips.

You inside my mind,
your head angled to one side.

Your eyes look across at me,
augers of emotion yet to come.

This feeling always present
along the length of my spine

whenever I think of you,
not here.

How lost I feel,
how you feel the same.

The Time of Our Lives

The rain flowed sideways
across the carriage window,

towards her sitting there
staring straight ahead.

As if it was attracted to her sorrow,
as if the rainfall wept for her.

A secret only she and the rain shared,
until I looked into her eyes

and I too flowed sideways,
falling into her grace.

Ma Belle

England is a dull place
without you.

Are you still there
Ma Belle?

Look at me,
how I write in stanzas

like my thoughts
are fragmented

and I can't put together
a single paragraph.

What have you done
to my way of thinking?

What have I done
to you and me, no more?

I Met Her in a Nightclub

Tell me about your hand,
how it would feel holding mine.

How your warmth would feel
inside my blood.

The way you would squeeze my hand
for no reason

other than that feeling
inside your blood

whenever we hold hands
and our shoulders touch by chance.

Sleeper

The English countryside
flashes by too familiar

as I gaze out of the window,
thinking a different life.

If I were to travel Trans-Siberian
in a sleeping carriage from the past

it would only be with you
by my side.

As the steady rock of the train
and the creak of the woodwork

soothes us into talking
about all those things left unsaid.

And you in my arms,
your warmth inside my blood,

as we watch the Urals pass by
in a window of our own making.

Victoria Line

Pressed together, his breath hot
against the side of my face,

as her hand touches mine, briefly,
before it slides down the pole.

Eyes avoid contact, mine too,
as we isolate each other.

His fingers grip the rail,
sore and grazed and chewed.

And no one talks throughout,
as we sway in unison,

close in proximity
yet miles away in everything else.

I Still Hear Your Voice

I can smell the sea
and you, your scent.

How I used to follow it
from room to room to room.

And the breeze
walking along the promenade

it carries the water,
the salt, memories unfolding.

Let's go chase the tide,
let the beast run wild tonight.

You always used to say,
always by my side.

Bodies Lying in the Sand

I wanted to hold your hand
into the sea.

Sleeping in and out of
consciousness,

memories merge perplexed
with dreams and dreams and dreams.

And I don't know if you
are more than just a thought,

I dreamt up last night sleeping
with Radiohead and whisky on ice.

Yet how could I ever imagine
a taste as sweet as yours?

My tongue inside your mouth
that first time we sexed;

how you awakened feelings
deep inside me,

and how I held onto your hand
until you let go.

Wilding the Beast

With you
and cello string melancholia

chasing acoustic guitar melodies
inside my mind,

your mind too,
both hearing the call.

Beside the beach
at daybreak, noon and night.

Your taste,
then your hair, touching my face

as I seek your eyes
sometimes open, sometimes closed.

Breathing in your skin scent,
touching with fingertip and tongue,

wilding the beast
one more time with you.

The First Cigarette of the Day

She never wore any makeup
and the fur around her hood was matted,

her hair too, looked unkempt
and I wanted to understand her wildness

but she sat almost unmoving
throughout the journey.

It wasn't until later,
as we approached Oxford Circus,

that she smiled into the window
and her eyes, like a child's first experience,

were full of light
yet wild as the night.

Listening to Obel
for the remainder of the tube ride

her eyes remained with me
and afterwards,

afterwards I still see them,
wild and innocent and haunting.

Affects Profound

Your words reside inside me
like a beating life force

around my body,
my mind, my dreams.

I take them everywhere I go
so that when you are not with me

– it's a lie
and I can hear your voice,

your words, how they affect me,
sustaining who I am,

as if your voice is a calling
and your silence a bitter end.

Echoes

There is nothing else I can say,
thinking of you.

Even though
you are no longer with me,

there is still a part of you
here by my side.

It's not a physical thing,
more a peace of mind emotion

the you affect inside
that sits so easy within my skin,

like a first moment remembered,
the first time I ever heard you cry.

Making Up

She sits three seats up from me
applying lipstick,

watching herself in the blank screen
of her mobile phone.

The draft from the open door chills my ankles
and visualises my breath,

but it soon closes and thirty seconds later
the train begins to move.

She uses a small black brush
on her lashes,

staring now
into a tiny circular mirror.

A single eye
suddenly watches me intently

black lined, unblinking,
it knows me,

I can feel it eating part of who I am
– something lost forever,

like a child's innocence
taken when you are not watching.

Afraid You Are Not Real

Rain streamed
down the carriage window

sounding in my mind
a thousand raindrops against the glass.

I can still smell it in my mind,
that day

in the cafe,
cappuccino and toasted panini.

Your perfume
somewhere in the mix

and your skin scent
as you applied hand cream afterwards.

Then your lips against mine,
raindrops against glass

as it poured outside the cafe
somewhere in our past.

Gospel

This is not love,
or some other spiritual phenomenon.

I simply want to be with you
every minute of the day.

To hear your voice say my name,
see your eyes watch me in the morning,

to taste your tongue
inside my mouth at night.

I want to walk with you through the market
to stop at each stall,

taking in the scent of citrus, peony
and you.

No, this is not love,
this is emotion inside a shell.

This is me,
needing you by my side.

Hello, Goodbye

I missed you
on the answer machine.

Listening to your voice again
hesitant, like you don't want to speak.

How I wanted to hear more,
more than hello, goodbye.

I still know you,
how each inflection

says so much more
than any word you speak.

And afterwards, I kiss you
over and again,

as I replay your message, listening
to words you do not want to say.

Darker Than

I woke up watching the lines
as the train pulled out of Heywood Heath.

You had been with me
inside my mind while I slept,

dreaming things
I could never imagine.

You took me by the hand
and led me laughing into your darkness,

the place where you told me
he cut off his own ears.

And here I am indifferent,
my face pressed against the glass

while you are there,
screaming nightmares into my life.

Endings

Someone died today,
stepped in front of a train.

If I had been inside
her footsteps

I too would be free
instead of thinking

dark thoughts aloud,
of you and me and this music

playing inside my head
a polyphonic soundscape.

It reminds me of you,
of me.

How we stepped into the night,
listening to autumn leaves fall.

How they never landed
until we said goodbye.

Altercation

I think he is going to die today,
and you too will know loss.

I wonder if you and I
have done the right thing.

Thinking about you each moment,
more so than ever before,

you seem so different
in my mind's eye today.

You still taste the same –
still talk the same in your sleep,

it's more about the meaning
in those final words you speak;

more an understanding that I am no longer
who you want me to be.

Must be Done

I want to comfort you,
be with you, now that he has gone.

But it is so much harder to talk
than it ever was before.

Like you are retrograde,
having slipped so easily into a new hostility.

Perhaps I should wait,
give you time to grieve

and I would, I would,
if only I hadn't perceived that tone

the one called '*no-way back*',
the one that tore us apart.

Where Everyone Goes to be Alone

She stared out of the window,
I don't know what she saw.

Outside was black and wet,
the night concealed everything.

I watched her stroke her hair
over and again,

until her unblinking eyes
suddenly filled with tears

and I wanted to stroke her hair then
over and again,

but I continued to stare
at her reflection in the window,

enjoying the feel
of another's sorrow more so

than the thought of comforting her,
even if it meant stroking her hair.

When the train stopped at York
and she got off,

I felt empty craving her tears,
craving her sorrow,

wanting her to weep for me
like I never could.

Miss the Things That Grow

It was my dead father who greeted me
just before Newark

as the sway and sway of the empty carriage
lulled me into sleep.

I hadn't seen him for over thirty years,
not since he lay unmoving on the hospital bed

with my brother sitting opposite,
weeping tears unremitting.

While I wondered
about my lack of emotion or any kind of tear.

He waved at me with that easy smile on his face
as he rocked backwards and forwards

and I suddenly began to weep inside my dream
my belated song of lament,

its tardy arrival measured in decades,
his premature goodbye measured in regret.

Placed by the Gideons

And I felt cold,
though the hotel room was hot,

as I imagined an ending
where everything was nothing.

A dark place forlorn,
where being no more has no meaning.

I almost sank into insignificance then,
until I remembered the drawer,

the book inside
and lying on the bed reading

I was struck at how new it felt,
like I was the only one

who had ever opened its pages,
I alone, in the beginning and the end.

Except those who placed it there,
those who didn't want me to be isolated.

Years ago – like the boy who made a promise
to his dying mother –

I too made a vow,
and right now, reading my undertaking

the hotel room remains the same,
but I no longer feel the cold.

Belongs to You and Me

Sitting alone
in the hotel restaurant,

all things considered
it's not so bad.

A blank page in front of me,
Pinot sitting pretty and music all around.

But the duck is far too crispy,
the skin far too salty

and I wish I'd chosen
something else instead.

You by my side
this life I now live forsaken.

Roadster

It was like stepping into a box,
a time capsule of the mind.

Me and the night-time air
with cars passing by occasionally

and each time they did
opportunity's door opened, beckoned.

Sitting on the wall
by the side of the road

inside my box,
listening to the guttural sound of death;

release,
pass on by like an alternative

where a choice could be made
and life silenced forever.

Make it Stop

We are alone
at all the important moments.

Each time we close our eyes,
each time we go to sleep.

And we have no control,
over anything of substance.

Don't close your eyes tonight,
don't go to sleep.

How I Mean Nothing to You

Things aren't quite right inside this place
but there is nothing I can do.

Thinking about everyone I have ever known
there is no one else I want to speak to but you.

Everything is painted black
come back, come back.

You see it creeps upon me,
this feeling of you

and I try not to think about the Camellia,
how its flower dropped whole from the stem,

instant and final inside your garden,
your garden, like a severed head alone.

Beautiful Lie

No one wants to die alone
but I see no other way.

I have always treasured you
though you will never know,

as you die amongst family
and friends, in a life I cannot share.

And I could alter the ending
live a beautiful lie with another,

but I will always love you,
I see no other way.

The Night Before

An empty hotel restaurant,
me and me forlorn.

The waiter places the jug of iced water
on the perfectly smooth tablecloth.

He remains professional,
non-judgemental.

While Mr Martin tells me to '*watch out*'
from unseen speakers.

I stare at the two tired buns
and the butter in the serving dish

thinking about this time of year
how it cuts so deeply

as Dean continues to sing
about someone '*coming home*'.

Everlasting, Without Asking

I cut it on the broken window,
the one I never got around to fixing.

Blood oozed slowly from the wound
and you wiped it with a damp cloth.

As my wrist continued to bleed
you licked it laboriously,

unconcerned, twice more,
pressing your tongue against my skin

until eventually
it bled no more.

How I need you here tonight
to do the same again.